THE OUTSIDERS

S. E. Hinton

EDITORIAL DIRECTOR Justin Kestler
EXECUTIVE EDITOR Ben Florman
DIRECTOR OF TECHNOLOGY Tammy Hepps

SERIES EDITORS John Crowther, Justin Kestler
MANAGING EDITOR Vince Janoski

WRITERS Brian Phillips, Shanti Sekaran
EDITORS Dennis Quinio, Emma Chastain

Copyright © 2002 by SparkNotes LLC

All rights reserved. No part of this book may be used or reproduced in any manner whatsoever without the written permission of the Publisher.

SPARKNOTES is a registered trademark of SparkNotes LLC

This edition published by Spark Publishing

Spark Publishing
A Division of SparkNotes LLC
120 Fifth Avenue, 8th Floor
New York, NY 10011

Any book purchased without a cover is stolen property, reported as "unsold and destroyed" to the Publisher, who receives no payment for such "stripped books."

Please submit all comments and questions or report errors to www.sparknotes.com/errors

Printed and bound in the United States

ISBN 1-58663-484-4

Introduction: Stopping to Buy SparkNotes on a Snowy Evening

Whose words these are you *think* you know.
Your paper's due tomorrow, though;
We're glad to see you stopping here
To get some help before you go.

Lost your course? You'll find it here.
Face tests and essays without fear.
Between the words, good grades at stake:
Get great results throughout the year.

Once school bells caused your heart to quake
As teachers circled each mistake.
Use SparkNotes and no longer weep,
Ace every single test you take.

Yes, books are lovely, dark, and deep,
But only what you grasp you keep,
With hours to go before you sleep,
With hours to go before you sleep.

Contents

CONTEXT	1
PLOT OVERVIEW	3
CHARACTER LIST	7
ANALYSIS OF MAJOR CHARACTERS	11
PONYBOY CURTIS	11
JOHNNY CADE	11
CHERRY VALANCE	12
THEMES, MOTIFS & SYMBOLS	15
BRIDGING THE GAP BETWEEN RICH AND POOR	15
HONOR AMONG THE LAWLESS	15
THE TREACHEROUSNESS OF MALE-FEMALE INTERACTIONS	16
LITERATURE	16
EYE SHAPE AND COLOR	17
PONYBOY'S LOSSES OF CONSCIOUSNESS	17
TWO-BIT'S SWITCHBLADE	17
CARS	18
BOB'S RINGS	18
GREASER HAIR	18
SUMMARY & ANALYSIS	19
CHAPTERS 1–2	19
CHAPTERS 3–4	22
CHAPTERS 5–6	25
CHAPTERS 7–8	28
CHAPTERS 9–10	31
CHAPTERS 11–12	33

IMPORTANT QUOTATIONS EXPLAINED   37

KEY FACTS   43

STUDY QUESTIONS & ESSAY TOPICS   45

REVIEW & RESOURCES   49
    QUIZ   49
    SUGGESTIONS FOR FURTHER READING   54

Context

SUSAN ELOISE HINTON WAS BORN in the 1950s in Tulsa, Oklahoma, a place that she describes as "a pleasant place to live if you don't want to do anything." She began *The Outsiders* at the age of fifteen, inspired by her frustration with the social divisions in her high school and the lack of realistic fiction for high school readers. *The Outsiders*, first published in 1967, tells the story of class conflict between the greasers, a group of low-class youths, and the Socs (short for Socials), a group of privileged rich kids who live on the wealthy West Side of town. The novel broke ground in the genre of Young Adult fiction, transcending established boundaries in its portrayal of violence, class conflict, and prejudice.

Hinton's publishers decided that Hinton should publish her novel under the name S. E. Hinton in order to cloak her gender. They worried that readers would not respect *The Outsiders*, which features male protagonists and violent situations, if they knew a female wrote it. Hinton has said that she does not mind using an authorial name that is gender neutral.

The language and details of the novel root the story in the sixties. Characters call fights "rumbles," and people listen to the Beatles and Elvis Presley. The novel is set in the Southwest, as evidenced by the fact that many greasers ride in local rodeos. Despite its location in a specific time and place, however, the novel is remarkable for its ability to transcend location. *The Outsiders* examines the universal urge to form factions, compete, and unite for survival. With only a few minor cosmetic changes, the novel could easily take place in a contemporary setting. This fact has given it universal appeal for the last few decades.

Hinton attempts to humanize the greasers, the outsiders of the story's title, by showing that their exterior toughness masks vulnerability and emotion. She makes both the greasers and the Socs sympathetic and refuses to cast blame on one group over the other. As one character tells another, "Things are rough all over."

After the publication of her first novel, Hinton felt pressure to turn out a successful sophomore effort. She had difficulty writing under this stress, and her boyfriend (who later become her husband) nudged her along by taking her out only if she had completed two pages per day. Hinton successfully finished her second novel, titled *That Was Then, This is Now,* published in 1971. In all, she has written eight novels for young adults. *The Outsiders* is Hinton's best-selling novel. A film version of the novel, starring C. Thomas Howell, Patrick Swayze, Emilio Estevez, Tom Cruise, Matt Dillon, Rob Lowe, and Ralph Macchio, was released in 1983.

Plot Overview

Ponyboy Curtis belongs to a lower-class group of Oklahoma youths who call themselves greasers because of their greasy long hair. Walking home from a movie, Ponyboy is attacked by a group of Socs, the greasers' rivals, who are upper-class youths from the West Side of town. The Socs, short for Socials, gang up on Ponyboy and threaten to slit his throat. A group of greasers comes and chases the bullies away, saving Ponyboy. Ponyboy's rescuers include his brother Sodapop, a charming, handsome high-school dropout, and Darry, Ponyboy's oldest brother (Darry assumed responsibility for his brothers when their parents were killed in a car crash). The rest of the greasers who come to Ponyboy's rescue are Johnny, a sensitive sixteen-year-old; Dally, a hardened street hood with a long criminal record; Steve, Sodapop's best friend; and Two-Bit, the oldest and funniest group member.

The next night, Ponyboy and Johnny go to a movie with Dally. They sit behind a pair of attractive Soc girls. Dally flirts with the girls obnoxiously. After Johnny tells Dally to stop harassing the Soc girls, Dally walks away. Johnny and Ponyboy sit with the girls, who are named Cherry and Marcia, and Ponyboy and Cherry discover that they have a lot in common. Two-Bit arrives, and the three greasers begin to walk the Soc girls to Two-Bit's house so he can drive them home. On the way to Two-Bit's house, they run into Bob and Randy, the girls' drunken boyfriends. The girls must leave with their boyfriends in order to prevent a fight between the Socs and the greasers.

Ponyboy is late getting home, and his brother Darry is furious with him. Sick of Darry's constant scrutiny and criticism, Ponyboy yells at Darry. The brothers begin to fight, and Darry slaps Ponyboy across the face. Ponyboy flees, determined to run away. He finds Johnny, and the two boys heads for the park. There they encounter Bob and Randy with a group of Soc boys. The Socs attack the Johnny and Ponyboy, and one of them holds Ponyboy's head under the frigid water of a fountain until Ponyboy blacks out. Ponyboy regains consciousness to find himself lying on the ground. He is next to Johnny—and next to Bob's corpse. Johnny tells Ponyboy that he (Johnny) killed Bob because the Socs were going to drown Ponyboy and beat up Johnny.

Desperate and terrified, Ponyboy and Johnny hurry to find Dally Winston, the one person they think might be able to help them. Dally gives them a gun and some money and sends them to an abandoned church near the neighboring town of Windrixville. They hide out in the church for a week, cutting and dying their hair to disguise themselves, reading *Gone with the Wind* aloud, and discussing poetry. After several days, Dally comes to check on Ponyboy and Johnny. He tells the boys that, since Bob's death, tensions between the greasers and the Socs have escalated. A rumble is to take place the next night to settle matters. He says that Cherry, who feels partially responsible for Bob's death, has been acting as a spy for the greasers. Johnny shocks Dally by declaring his intention to go back and turn himself in.

Dally agrees to drive Ponyboy and Johnny back home. However, as the boys leave, they notice that the abandoned church where Ponyboy and Johnny have been staying has caught fire. They discover that a group of schoolchildren has wandered inside. Ponyboy and Johnny rush into the inferno to save the children. Just as they get the last child through the window, the roof caves in, and Ponyboy blacks out. He regains consciousness in an ambulance. At the hospital, he is diagnosed with minor burns and bruises. Dally is not badly hurt either, but Johnny's back was broken by the falling roof, and he is in critical condition. Darry and Sodapop come to get Ponyboy, and Darry and Ponyboy make up. The following morning, the newspapers proclaim Ponyboy and Johnny heroes. They also report that, because of Bob's death, Johnny will be charged with manslaughter. Finally, the papers also state that both Ponyboy and Johnny will have to go to juvenile court so that a judge can decide if they should be sent to a boys' home.

Ponyboy and Two-Bit go to get a Coke and run into Randy. Randy tells Ponyboy that he is sick of all the fighting and does not plan to go to the rumble that night. When Ponyboy and Two-Bit visit Johnny in the hospital, Johnny seems weak. He asks Ponyboy for a new copy of *Gone with the Wind*. During their visit with Dally, Ponyboy and Two-Bit notice that Dally is much stronger than Johnny. Dally asks to borrow Two-Bit's black-handled switchblade. On the way home, Two-Bit and Ponyboy see Cherry. She refuses to visit Johnny because he has killed Bob, and Ponyboy calls her a traitor. When she explains herself, he relents.

At the rumble, the greasers defeat the Socs. Dally shows up just in time for the fight; he has escaped from the hospital. After the fight,

Ponyboy and Dally hurry back to see Johnny and find that he is dying. When Johnny dies, Dally loses control and runs from the room in a frenzy. Ponyboy stumbles home late that night, feeling dazed and disoriented. He tells the others of Johnny's death. Dally calls to say that he has robbed a grocery store and the cops are looking for him. The greasers hurry to find him, but they are too late. Dally raises a gun to the police and they gun him down. Overwhelmed, Ponyboy passes out.

Ponyboy wakes up in bed at home. He has suffered a concussion from a kick to the head at the rumble and has been delirious in bed for several days. When he is well, he attends his hearing, where the judge treats him kindly and acquits him of responsibility for Bob's death. The court rules that Ponyboy will be allowed to remain at home with Darry. For a time, Ponyboy feels listless and empty. His grades slip, he feels hostile to Darry, and he loses his appetite. At last, Sodapop tells Ponyboy that he (Sodapop) is angry and frustrated because of the tension at home. He tearfully asks that Ponyboy and Darry stop fighting. Finally understanding the value of his family, Ponyboy agrees not to fight with Darry anymore. He finds that for the first time he can remember Dally's and Johnny's deaths without pain or denial. He decides to tell their story and begins writing a term paper for his English class, which turns out to be the novel itself.

Character List

Ponyboy Curtis The novel's fourteen-year-old narrator and protagonist, and the youngest of the greasers. Ponyboy's literary interests and academic accomplishments set him apart from the rest of his gang. Because his parents have died in a car accident, Ponyboy lives with his brothers Darry and Sodapop. Darry repeatedly accuses Ponyboy of lacking common sense, but Ponyboy is a reliable and observant narrator. Throughout the novel, Ponyboy struggles with class division, violence, innocence, and familial love. He matures over the course of the novel, eventually realizing the importance of strength in the face of class bias.

Darrell Curtis Ponyboy's oldest brother. Darrell, known as "Darry," is a twenty-year-old greaser who is raising Ponyboy because their parents have died in a car crash. Strong, athletic, and intelligent, Darry has quit school. He works two jobs to hold the family together. The unofficial leader of the greasers, he becomes an authority figure for Ponyboy. He also makes good chocolate cake, which he and his brothers eat every day for breakfast. The other greasers call him "Superman."

Sodapop Curtis Ponyboy's happy-go-lucky, handsome brother. Sodapop is the middle Curtis boy. Ponyboy envies Sodapop's good looks and charm. Sodapop plans to marry Sandy, a greaser girl.

Two-Bit Mathews The joker of Ponyboy's group. Two-Bit, whose real name is Keith, is a wisecracking greaser who regularly shoplifts. He prizes his sleek black-handled switchblade. He instigates the hostilities between the Socs and the greasers by flirting with Marcia, the girlfriend of a Soc.

Steve Randle Sodapop's best friend since grade school. Steve is a seventeen-year-old greaser who works with Sodapop at the gas station. Steve knows everything about cars and specializes in stealing hubcaps. He is cocky and intelligent, tall and lean. He wears his thick hair in a complicated arrangement of swirls. He is also tough— he once held off four opponents in a fight with a broken soda bottle. He sees Ponyboy as Sodapop's annoying kid brother and wishes Ponyboy would not tag along so often.

Dallas Winston The toughest hood in Ponyboy's group of greasers. Dallas, known as "Dally," is a hardened teen who used to run with gangs in New York. He has an elfin face and icy blue eyes and, unlike his friends, does not put grease in his white-blond hair. Dally's violent tendencies make him more dangerous than the other greasers, and he takes pride in his criminal record. Dally feels protective of Johnny Cade.

Johnny Cade A sixteen-year-old greaser with black hair and large, fearful eyes. Though Johnny does not succeed in school, he approaches intellectual matters with steady concentration. The child of alcoholic, abusive parents, he is nervous and sensitive. Since his parents do not care for him, Johnny sees the greasers as his true family. In turn, the older boys, particularly Dally, are protective of him.

Sandy Sodapop's girlfriend. Sandy is pregnant with another man's child and moves to Florida to live with her grandmother. Like the other greaser girls, Sandy appears in the text only when the boys mention her.

Cherry Valance Bob's girlfriend, she is a Soc cheerleader whom Ponyboy meets at the movies. Cherry's real name is Sherry, but people call her Cherry because of her red hair. Ponyboy and Cherry have a great deal in common, and Ponyboy feels comfortable talking to her. Cherry is both offended and intrigued by her encounter with

Dally Winston at the drive-in. Cherry admires Dally's individuality and tells Ponyboy that she could fall in love with Dally. In the days preceding the rumble, Cherry becomes a spy for the greasers.

Marcia   Cherry's friend and Randy's girlfriend. Marcia is a pretty, dark-haired Soc who befriends Two-Bit at the drive-in. Marcia and Two-Bit share a sense of humor and a taste for nonsensical musings.

Randy Anderson Marcia's boyfriend and Bob's best friend. Randy is a handsome Soc who eventually sees the futility of fighting. Along with Cherry, Randy humanizes the Socs by showing that some of them have redeeming qualities. Randy helps Ponyboy realize that Socs are as susceptible to pain as anyone else. Randy tries to make peace with Ponyboy after Ponyboy saves the children from the fire, and he refuses to fight in the Soc-greaser rumble.

Bob Sheldon Cherry's boyfriend. Bob is the dark-haired Soc who beats up Johnny before the novel begins. Bob has a set of three heavy rings, which he wears when he fights greasers. Bob's indulgent parents have never disciplined him.

Paul Holden The husky blond Soc who steps forward to challenge Darry when the rumble begins. Paul and Darry were friends and football teammates in high school.

Jerry Wood The teacher who accompanies Ponyboy to the hospital after Ponyboy saves the children from the fire. Though an adult and a member of mainstream society, Jerry judges the greasers on their merits instead of automatically branding them juvenile delinquents.

Tim Shepard The leader of another band of greasers and a friend of Dally. Tim and Dally respect each other, despite occasional conflicts. Ponyboy thinks of Tim as an alley cat, hungry and restless. Tim does not appear in the novel until the night of the rumble, when his gang sides with Ponyboy's. Ponyboy sees Shepard's gang as real street hoods and criminals, and realizes that his own gang is little more than a group of friends fighting to survive.

Curly Shepard The fifteen-year-old brother of Tim Shepard. Curly is stubborn and rough. He cannot go to the rumble because he was put in a reformatory for six months after robbing a liquor store. Tim is proud of Curly's criminal record.

Mr. Syme Ponyboy's English teacher. Mr. Syme expresses concern over Ponyboy's falling grades. He offers to raise Ponyboy's grade if he turns in a well-written autobiographical theme. This assignment inspires Ponyboy to write about the greasers and the Socs, and his autobiographical theme turns into the novel *The Outsiders*.

Analysis of Major Characters

Ponyboy Curtis

Ponyboy Curtis, the youngest member of the greasers, narrates the novel. Ponyboy theorizes on the motivations and personalities of his friends and describes events in a slangy, youthful voice. Though only fourteen years old, he understands the way his social group functions and the role each group member plays. He sees that Two-Bit is the wisecracker, Darry the natural leader, and Dally the dangerous hood.

Ponyboy dislikes the Socs, whom we see through his subjective viewpoint. The distorting effects of hatred and group rivalry make his narration less than objective. Ponyboy is young enough to have changeable conceptions of people, however, and over the course of the novel he realizes that Socs have problems just as greasers do. He also comes to see that Socs are even similar to the greasers in some ways.

Ponyboy has a literary bent, which Hinton uses to show that poverty does not necessarily mean boorishness or lack of culture, and that gang members are not always delinquents. Ponyboy identifies with Pip, the impoverished protagonist of Charles Dickens's *Great Expectations*, cites the Robert Frost poem "Nothing Gold Can Stay," and introduces Johnny to the southern gentlemen of Margaret Mitchell's Southern epic, *Gone with the Wind*. With such an awareness of literary protagonists, Ponyboy sees himself as he is, as both character and narrator. He takes on the narrator's work of recounting events and the character's work of growing and changing as a result of those events. The novel is not just a story of gang rivalry; it is an account of Ponyboy's development.

Johnny Cade

Johnny Cade is a vulnerable sixteen-year-old greaser in a group defined by toughness and a sense of invincibility. He comes from an abusive home, and he takes to the greasers because they are his only reliable family. While Johnny needs the greasers, the greasers also need Johnny, for protecting him gives them a sense of purpose and justifies their violent measures. When Johnny, little and vulnerable, suffers at the hands of the Socs, the greasers feel justified in their hatred of the rival gang.

Passive and quiet, Johnny is the principal catalyst for the major events of the novel. He stands up to Dally at the drive-in and tells him to stop harassing the two Soc girls, Cherry and Marcia. Johnny's intervention on the girls' behalf pleases the girls, and they talk and walk with the greasers. This interaction between female Socs and male greasers sparks the anger of the Soc boys and motivates them to attack Johnny and Ponyboy. Ultimately, Johnny's small acts of courage lead to murder, death, and heroic rescue. But Johnny ends by advocating against gang violence, stating that he would gladly sacrifice his life for the lives of little children. Although a gentle boy, he has a profound impact with his startling, persistent demand for peace. His courage in rescuing the children from the burning church and his subsequent death as a result of injuries sustained in the rescue make him a martyr. Ponyboy's decision to write the story that becomes *The Outsiders* ensures that Johnny's bravery will not be forgotten.

CHERRY VALANCE

Before Cherry Valance enters the narrative, Ponyboy paints the conflict between the greasers and the Socs as irreconcilable. The introduction of Cherry, however, suggests that individual friendships can chip away at group hatreds. Cherry gets along perfectly well with some of the greasers. She likes Ponyboy and Johnny because they treat her politely. Dally's rude antics do not amuse her. Her disenchantment with Dally's behavior suggests that she talks to Ponyboy and Johnny not because she is slumming and their greaser identity fascinates her, but rather because she likes them as individuals. For a short while at least, she cares more about how each boy behaves than about his West Side or East Side address.

Cherry is not just a sweet, simple girl. She finds herself sexually attracted to Dally, who is crass and unrefined but also sexy and charismatic. Despite all her attraction to the greasers, moreover, she is not completely free of group prejudice. She tells Ponyboy she probably will not say hello to him at school, acknowledging that she respects social divisions. Although Cherry plays a relatively small role in the novel, the ambiguity of her sympathies gives us something to which we can relate. She mirrors our own perspective as someone close to the action who is nevertheless an outsider and who does not always fully understand other characters' emotions and motivations.

Themes, Motifs & Symbols

Themes

Themes are the fundamental and often universal ideas explored in a literary work.

Bridging the Gap Between Rich and Poor

The Outsiders tells the story of two groups of teenagers whose bitter rivalry stems from socioeconomic differences. However, Hinton suggests, these differences in social class do not necessarily make natural enemies of the two groups. The greasers and Socs share some things in common. Cherry Valance, a Soc, and Ponyboy Curtis, a greaser, discuss their shared love of literature, popular music, and sunsets, transcending—if only temporarily—the divisions that feed the feud between their respective groups. Their harmonious conversation suggests that shared passions can fill in the gap between rich and poor. This potential for agreement marks a bright spot in the novel's gloomy prognosis that the battle between the classes is a long-lasting one. Over the course of the novel, Ponyboy begins to see the pattern of shared experience. He realizes that the hardships that greasers and Socs face may take different practical forms, but that the members of both groups—and youths everywhere—must inevitably come to terms with fear, love, and sorrow.

Honor Among the Lawless

The idea of honorable action appears throughout the novel, and it works as an important component of the greaser behavioral code. Greasers see it as their duty, Ponyboy says, to stand up for each other in the face of enemies and authorities. In particular, we see acts of honorable duty from Dally Winston, a character who is primarily defined by his delinquency and lack of refinement. Ponyboy informs us that once, in a show of group solidarity, Dally let himself be arrested for a crime that Two-Bit had committed. Furthermore, when discussing *Gone with the Wind,* Johnny says that he views Dally as a Southern gentleman, as a man with a fixed personal code of behavior. Statements like Johnny's, coupled with acts of honorable sacrifice throughout the narrative, demonstrate that courtesy and propriety can exist even among the most lawless of social groups.

The Treacherousness of Male-Female Interactions

As hostile and dangerous as the greaser-Soc rivalry becomes, the boys from each group have the comfort of knowing how their male friends will react to their male enemies. When Randy and Bob approach Ponyboy and Johnny, everyone involved knows to expect a fight of some sort. It is only when the female members of the Soc contingent start to act friendly toward the greasers that animosities blur and true trouble starts brewing. Even on the greaser side, Sodapop discovers female unreliability when he finds out that his girlfriend is pregnant with another man's child. With these plot elements, Hinton conveys the idea that cross-gender interaction creates unpredictable results. This message underscores the importance of male bonding in the novel to the creation of unity and structure.

Motifs

Motifs are recurring structures, contrasts, or literary devices that can help to develop and inform the text's major themes.

Literature

Literary references occur throughout *The Outsiders*, helping us understand how the characters in the novel view themselves and those around them. Ponyboy first alludes to a work of literature in Chapter 1, when he compares himself to Pip from Charles Dickens's *Great Expectations*. Ponyboy identifies with Pip because he, like Pip, is orphaned, impoverished, and struggling to make sense of the world. Additionally Ponyboy and Johnny put special emphasis on Robert Frost's poem "Nothing Gold Can Stay," which helps them understand that growing up and facing reality is a necessary part of life. Finally, Johnny likens Dally to a Southern gentleman in *Gone with the Wind*. Having this idealized vision of Dally makes Johnny able to understand him.

Literature not only creates a bond between Ponyboy and the other characters, as when he discusses books with Cherry and reads to Johnny, but it also creates a cyclic premise for the narrative itself. We find out at the novel's end that the narrative of *The Outsiders* is in fact an autobiographical work that Ponyboy is writing in order to pass his English class. This revelation confirms the importance of literature in the story as a means of connecting with others.

Eye Shape and Color

Though Hinton gives thorough physical descriptions of all her characters, she places particular importance on their eyes. Characters' eyes represent key facets of their personalities. For example, Darry and Dally—the two boys with whom Ponyboy feels the least comfortable—have icy blue eyes. Dally's eyes, in particular, are narrow. The narrator considers these two characters to be hard, even heartless, and the narrowness and cool hues of their eyes reflect their invulnerability. Hinton repeatedly defines Johnny Cade, on the other hand, by his wide, brown eyes. In correspondence with his eye shape and color, Johnny is generally nervous, gentle, and vulnerable to attack.

Ponyboy's Losses of Consciousness

During the second half of the novel, beginning with the scene at the burning church, Ponyboy loses consciousness multiple times. It might seem strange at first to have a narrator slip in and out of mental clarity and thus miss out on entire spans of plot development. However, it makes sense that Hinton would distance her narrator temporarily in this manner, as this gives us, as well as Ponyboy, a needed rest from the intense action. This device also allows for events to be recounted after they happen, so that Ponyboy can sift through unnecessary details.

Symbols

Symbols are objects, characters, figures, or colors used to represent abstract ideas or concepts.

Two-Bit's Switchblade

Two-Bit's switchblade is his most prized possession and, in several ways, represents the disregard for authority for which greasers traditionally pride themselves. First of all, the blade is stolen. Second, it represents a sense of the individual power that comes with the potential to commit violence. This symbolism surfaces most clearly when Dally borrows the blade from Two-Bit and uses it to break out of the hospital to join his gang at the rumble. It is fitting that Two-Bit finally loses the blade when the police confiscate it from Dally's dead body. The loss of the weapon, at this point, becomes inextricably linked with the loss of Dally—a figure who embodies individual power and authority.

Cars

Cars represent the Socs power and the greasers' vulnerability. Because their parents can afford to buy them their "tuff" cars, the Socs have increased mobility and protection. The greasers, who move mostly on foot, are physically vulnerable in comparison to the Socs. Still, greasers like Darry, Sodapop, and Steve do have contact with automobiles—they repair them. We can interpret this interaction with cars positively or negatively. On one hand, it symbolizes how the greasers have a more direct and well-rounded experience than the Socs with the gritty realities of life. On the other hand, the fact that the greasers must service and care for Soc possessions demonstrates that the Socs have the power to oppress the greasers.

Bob's Rings

Bob Sheldon's rings function similarly to the Socs' cars. Throughout literature, rings and jewelry have been traditional symbols of wealth. The rings in this story represent the physical power that accompanies wealth. By using his rings as combative weapons, Bob takes advantage of his economic superiority over Ponyboy and the other greasers, using his wealth to injure his opponents.

Greaser Hair

The greasers cannot afford rings, cars, or other physical trappings of power that the Socs enjoy. Consequently, they must resort to more affordable markers of identity. By wearing their hair in a specific style, greasers distinguish themselves from other social groups. Conservative cultural values of the 1960s called for men to keep their hair short, and the greaser style is a clear transgression of this social convention. It is not only distinctive, but, as a physical characteristic, this hair is truly an organic part of the greaser persona. When the Socs jump Ponyboy at the beginning of the novel, they ask him if he wants a haircut and threaten to cut off his hair. By doing so, they would rob him of his identity.

Summary & Analysis

Chapters 1–2

Summary: Chapter 1

Ponyboy Curtis, the narrator, begins the novel with a story: he is walking home one afternoon after watching a Paul Newman film, and his mind starts to wander. He thinks about how he wants Paul Newman's good looks, though he likes his own greaser look. He also thinks that, although he likes to watch movies alone, he wishes he had company for the walk home.

Ponyboy steps back from his story to explain that walking alone is unsafe for greasers, the East Side gang of friends to which he belongs. When they walk by themselves, greasers attract the harassment of Socials, or Socs, the rich West Side crowd. Ponyboy says that greasers are poorer and wilder than the Socs, whom the newspapers condemn one day for throwing parties and praise the next day for good citizenship. Greasers wear their hair long and put grease in it. They dress tough, steal, and get into gang fights. They often carry switchblades, mainly to help them stand their ground against the Socs.

Ponyboy says he does not participate in typical greaser mischief because his oldest brother, Darrell (known as "Darry"), would kill him if he got into trouble. Ponyboy's parents died in a car crash, so the three Curtis brothers live together by themselves, an arrangement possible only as long as they stay out of trouble. Twenty-year-old Darry acts as head of the family. He is strict with Ponyboy and often yells at him. Despite his intelligence, Ponyboy lacks common sense, which frustrates Darry. Ponyboy feels great affection for his sixteen-year-old brother, Sodapop, whose charm and cheerfulness he admires.

Ponyboy returns to the story of his solitary walk after the movies. As he walks, he notices a red Corvair trailing him. He quickens his pace as he remembers how badly the Socs beat his friend Johnny Cade. The Corvair pulls up beside Ponyboy and five Socs climb out and surround him. One of them asks, "Need a haircut, greaser?" and pulls out a blade. The Socs begin to beat up Ponyboy, who screams for help. Ponyboy's brothers and the rest of their group appear on the scene and chase away the Socs. Darry starts to scold Ponyboy for walking home alone instead of calling for a ride, but Sodapop tells him to stop nagging.

The brothers and the other greasers and make plans for the following night. Ponyboy decides that he and Johnny will go to a double feature at the drive-in with their friend Dally. Dally begins to talk about his ex-girlfriend, Sylvia, and Ponyboy thinks about the girls that socialize with the greasers. He wonders what it would be like to spend time with an upper-class Soc girl.

At home, Ponyboy, who loves to read, reads *Great Expectations* and thinks about how his life resembles the life of Pip, the main character in *Great Expectations*. Still shaken by his fight with the Socs, Ponyboy climbs into bed with Sodapop. The brothers talk about Sodapop's girlfriend, Sandy, whom Sodapop hopes to marry one day.

Summary: Chapter 2

The next night, Ponyboy and Johnny go with Dally to a double feature at the drive-in movie theater. They sit behind a pair of Soc girls, and Dally begins to talk dirty in an attempt to embarrass the girls. The girl with red hair turns around and coolly tells him to stop, but Dally continues to make suggestive remarks. He goes to buy Cokes, and Ponyboy talks to the red-haired girl, Cherry Valance. They talk about the rodeo and about Sodapop, whom Cherry describes as a "doll." She asks what became of Sodapop, and although the admission embarrasses him, Ponyboy says that Sodapop dropped out of school to work in a gas station. Cherry and her friend Marcia invite Ponyboy and Johnny to watch the movie with them. Dally comes back and offers a Coke to Cherry, but she throws it in his face. Dally tries to put his arm around her. When he will not listen to Cherry's protests, the usually quiet Johnny stuns Dally by telling him not to bother the girls.

Dally stalks off, and the boys sit with the girls and watch the movie. Two-Bit, one of Ponyboy's friends, comes to announce that Dally has slashed Tim Shepard's tires and is going to have to fight him. Tim Shepard is the leader of another greaser gang. Two-Bit explains the greasers' two main rules: always stick together and never get caught.

Cherry and Ponyboy go to get popcorn, and Ponyboy tells her about the time the Socs beat up Johnny. The leader of the gang that beat him, Ponyboy says, wore a fistful of rings. Cherry looks distressed and assures him that not all Socs are violent like the Socs that beat Johnny. She also tells him that Socs have problems just as the greasers do, but Ponyboy does not believe her.

Analysis: Chapters 1–2

The Outsiders' primary concern is to explore the effect of social class on young people. The novel begins by detailing the differences between the poor greasers and the rich Socs and sketching the treacherous world in which they live. When the Socs jump Ponyboy in the opening chapter, it suggests that Ponyboy lives in a place where even an innocent walk is fraught with danger.

Hinton defines her characters as she thinks people should be defined in life—not according to the group to which they belong, but according to their individual characteristics. For instance, she introduces Ponyboy not as a tough street youth but as a boy who likes to read and watch sunsets. Ponyboy is something of an anthropologist, a natural role for a narrator, and he observes and records the group dynamics and individual traits of his fellow greasers. Darry is presented not as the natural leader of the gang, but as a struggling young man who has had to forgo an education so that he can support and raise his two younger brothers. Hinton suggests that greasers, despite their exclusion from the mainstream, have moral grounding and sense of decency as strong as—or stronger than—the kids from the privileged classes.

Hinton shows the constant conflict between the greasers and the Socs, but she also shows that the two groups are not as different as they initially appear. After meeting faceless, cruel Socs, we meet Cherry Valance, a Soc who is also a sympathetic, warm girl. She and Ponyboy discuss how greasers and Socs deal with their problems differently. Greasers feel their distress keenly, while Socs pretend their problems do not exist. Ponyboy's and Cherry's discussion reveals that, despite different methods of coping, both Socs and greasers must deal with difficulties. The conversation between Cherry and Ponyboy exemplifies the rare civil negotiation that would alleviate the tensions between the Socs and greasers far more than violent conflict. The flirtation between Two-Bit and Marcia demonstrates the social compatibility that could exist between the warring groups.

Hinton suggests that male-female friendships are the friendships most likely to result in peace between the groups. In the first half of the novel, all encounters between male greasers and male Socs result in violence, whereas encounters between male greasers and female Socs sometimes end in laughter and flirtation. This difference suggests that gang rivalry stems from male hatred of other males. Conversely, the strongly masculine nature of the rivalry means that internal group bonding is also strongly masculine. Female greasers essentially do not exist in this novel; they are discussed, but they never appear as characters. Their absence emphasizes the intense male bonding among the greasers.

In the Young Adult fiction genre, *The Outsiders* is unique in its early suggestion that the rival groups are not that different from each other. By establishing this commonality at the beginning, Hinton throws us off balance. That Hinton raises the possibility of resolution between gangs so early but delays resolution for so long keeps the focus on the individual issues that Ponyboy and others face.

Chapters 3–4

Summary: Chapter 3

Just don't forget that some of us watch the sunset too.
(See QUOTATIONS, p. 38)

Ponyboy, Two-Bit, and Johnny walk to Two-Bit's house with Cherry and Marcia so that they can give the girls a ride home. As they walk, Ponyboy and Cherry talk about Ponyboy's brothers. He notices how easy it is to talk to Cherry. When Cherry asks Ponyboy to describe Darry, he says Darry does not like him and probably wishes he could put Ponyboy in a home somewhere. Johnny and Two-Bit are startled to hear that Ponyboy feels this way, and Johnny says he always thought the three brothers got along well.

After Ponyboy tells Cherry about Sodapop's old horse, Mickey Mouse, the two move on to discuss the differences they perceive between Socs and greasers. During this discussion, Ponyboy and Cherry find they have a surprising amount in common—for instance, they both like reading and watching sunsets. Ponyboy voices his frustration that the greasers have terrible luck while the Socs lead comfortable lives and jump the greasers out of sheer boredom. Cherry retorts that the Socs' situations are not as simple as Ponyboy thinks. They decide that the main difference between Socs and greasers is that Socs are too cool and aloof to acknowledge their emotions and that they live their lives trying to fill up their emotional void, while the greasers feel everything too intensely. Ponyboy realizes that, although they come from different classes, he and Cherry watch the same sunset.

A blue Mustang cruises by the group. The Mustang belongs to Bob and Randy, Cherry's and Marcia's Soc boyfriends. The Mustang pulls up beside the group, and Randy and Bob get out. Ponyboy notices that Bob wears three heavy rings on his hand. The greasers and Socs nearly get into a fight, but the girls agree to leave with their boyfriends to prevent violence. Before leaving, Cherry tells Ponyboy that she hopes she won't see Dally again, because she thinks she could fall in love with him.

Ponyboy walks home and finds Darry furious with him for staying out so late. In the ensuing argument, Darry slaps Ponyboy. No one in Ponyboy's family has ever hit him before, and Ponyboy storms out of the house in a rage. He feels sure now that Darry does not want him around. It is after two o'clock in the morning. Ponyboy finds Johnny in the lot where the greasers hang out, and he tells Johnny that they are running away. Johnny, who lives with his abusive alcoholic father, agrees to run away without hesitating. The boys decide to walk through the park and determine whether they really want to leave.

Summary: Chapter 4

The park is deserted at 2:30 in the morning. Ponyboy and Johnny go walking beside the fountain. It is cold out, and Ponyboy is wearing only a short-sleeved shirt. Suddenly the boys see the blue Mustang from earlier that night. Five Socs, including Randy and Bob, jump out of the car and approach them. Presumably, the Socs have come to get even with the boys for picking up their girlfriends. Ponyboy can tell they are drunk. Bob tells Ponyboy that greasers are white trash with long hair, and Ponyboy retorts that Socs are nothing but white trash with Mustangs and madras shirts. In a rage, Ponyboy spits at the Socs. A Soc grabs Ponyboy and holds his head under the frigid water of the fountain. Ponyboy feels himself drowning and blacks out. When he regains consciousness, the Socs have run away. He is lying on the pavement next to Johnny. Bob's bloody corpse is nearby. Johnny says, "I killed him," and Ponyboy sees Johnny's switchblade, dark to the hilt with blood.

Ponyboy panics, but Johnny remains calm. They decide to go to Dally, thinking he might be able to help them. They find Dally at the house of Buck Merril, his rodeo partner. He manages to get the boys fifty dollars, a change of clothing for Ponyboy, and a loaded gun. He instructs them to take a train to Windrixville, where they can hide in an abandoned church. Ponyboy and Johnny get on a train, and Ponyboy goes to sleep. When they get to Windrixville, they hop off the train and find the church, where they collapse into exhausted sleep.

Analysis: Chapters 3–4

In these chapters, Hinton uses symbols to represent the tensions between the two socioeconomic groups. The Socs' blue Mustang symbolizes their class and power, since a greaser could never afford such a "tuff car." The Mustang symbolizes the economic divide between the two groups and points to a major source of the tensions between them. In this section, and in most of the novel, the greasers move about on foot, leaving themselves vulnerable to the Socs, who are protected in their cars. Bob's ring collection is another material manifestation of the Socs' wealth and, by contrast, the greasers' poverty. Ponyboy identifies Bob, a Soc, by the large rings he wears on his fingers, and, of course, jewelry of this kind is a traditional symbol of wealth. But Bob also uses these rings as weapons in his attacks, in the same way that brass knuckles are used to increase the damage of a punch in a fight. Therefore, on a symbolic level, Bob transforms his wealth into a physical weapon. Greasers, on the other hand, cannot represent themselves with material luxuries. Their primary identifying symbol is their long hair. Unlike cars or rings, hair is a costless symbol, all the cheaper because the greasers do not have to pay to cut or style their hair. Cars and jewelry symbolize the Socs; hair symbolizes the greasers. These superficial features differentiate the two gangs, reinforcing the role that material acquisitions play in forging the novel's group identities.

This section introduces the novel's major crisis. When the Socs attack Ponyboy and Johnny, but they also are not only trespassing on greaser territory, they are starting an unfair fight and taking advantage of the boys' physical vulnerability. On a psychological level, this incident presents a crisis for Ponyboy because it casts doubt in his mind over the burgeoning conclusions he makes about the commonalities between the Socs and the greasers. Still, Hinton makes Johnny's killing of Bob morally uncomplicated. If Johnny had not attacked Bob, Ponyboy would have drowned. Although Johnny commits murder, he does not lose our sympathy. Hinton portrays him not as a killer but as a defender of his friend's life and a victim of tragic circumstance. His actions are regrettable, but his motives and values are noble—he wants to save his friend's life.

As a result of the murder, Johnny and Ponyboy attain a new status in the narrative, as well as among the greasers. Initially, both boys play passive roles in the narrative and in their social group. Ponyboy plays the role of an observer and is seen as a "tagalong," while Johnny rarely even speaks. By murdering a Soc, however, Johnny becomes an adult. He shows his strength when he remains calm after the murder and rationally determines a course of action. Ponyboy's proximity to the murder makes him important, not least because he unintentionally motivates Johnny to murder Bob. Accidentally, the two boys begin to take an active role in the story, instigating events, exacerbating tensions between the two gangs, and pushing the narrative forward.

CHAPTERS 5–6

SUMMARY: CHAPTER 5

Dally was so real he scared me.

(See QUOTATIONS, p. 39)

The next morning, Ponyboy wakes in the church and finds a note from Johnny saying that he has gone into town to get supplies. When Johnny returns, he brings a week's supply of bologna and cigarettes, and a paperback copy of *Gone with the Wind*, which he wants Ponyboy to read to him. Ponyboy makes a wisecrack and Johnny tells him he is becoming more like Two-Bit every day. Johnny insists that they cut their hair to disguise themselves, and he bleaches Ponyboy's hair.

For the next week, the boys hide out at the church, reading *Gone with the Wind*, smoking, and eating sandwiches. The boys admire the southern gentlemen in *Gone with the Wind*, and Johnny points out that they remind him of Dally. Ponyboy disagrees. He prefers the other greasers to Dally. Most of the greasers remind Ponyboy of the heroes in novels, but Dally is so real he is frightening. Later,

Ponyboy recites a Robert Frost poem, "Nothing Gold Can Stay." The poem touches Johnny.

After about five days, Dally shows up at the church with a letter to Ponyboy from Sodapop. Dally says the police approached him about Bob's murder and he told them that the perpetrators fled to Texas. He takes Johnny and Ponyboy to the Dairy Queen and tells them that a state of open warfare exists between the greasers and the Socs, who are furious about Bob's death. He also lets slip that Cherry Valance, feeling responsible for the murderous encounter, has been acting as a spy for the greasers. He adds that in a day's time the two groups will meet for a rumble.

Summary: Chapter 6

Johnny shocks Dally by telling him he wants to go back home and confess to his crime. Dally tries to change Johnny's mind, telling him he never wants to see Johnny hardened the way prison would harden him. Johnny is adamant and points out that his own parents would not care what happens to him, but Ponyboy's brothers care about him and want to see him. Swearing under his breath, Dally begins to drive Johnny and Ponyboy home. As they drive past the church where Ponyboy and Johnny have been staying, they see that it is on fire. Ponyboy thinks he and Johnny must have started the fire with a cigarette butt, so the boys jump out of the car to examine the blaze.

At the church, they find a group of schoolchildren on a picnic. Suddenly, one of the adult chaperones cries out that some of the children are missing, and Ponyboy hears screaming from inside the church. Acting on instinct, he and Johnny climb into the burning building through a window. At the back of the church, they find the children huddled together and terrified. As he runs through the smoky inferno, Ponyboy wonders why he is not scared. He and Johnny lift the children out of the window. Dally appears and yells that the roof is about to cave in. As they lift the last child out the window, the roof crumbles. Johnny pushes Ponyboy out of the window, and then Ponyboy hears Johnny scream. Ponyboy starts to go back in for Johnny, but Dally clubs him across the back and knocks him out.

When Ponyboy wakes, he is in an ambulance, accompanied by one of the schoolteachers, Jerry Wood. The teacher tells him that his back caught on fire and that the jacket he was wearing, which Dally lent him, saved his life. He says that Dally was burned but will probably be fine. Johnny, however, is in very bad shape—he was struck by a piece of burning timber as it fell, and may have broken his back. The man jokingly asks Ponyboy if he and Johnny are professional heroes. Ponyboy tells him that they are juvenile delinquents.

Ponyboy has suffered mild burns. Jerry stays with him while he is in the hospital, and Ponyboy confides the story of Bob's death. Jerry agrees that Johnny killed Bob in self-defense. He tells Ponyboy he shouldn't smoke, something that no one has ever said to Ponyboy before. Darry and Sodapop arrive. Sodapop hugs Ponyboy, and Darry cries, shocking Ponyboy. The anger he has felt toward Darry dissolves. Ponyboy realizes that Darry does care about him; Darry is strict because he loves Ponyboy and wants him to succeed. Ponyboy runs across the room and embraces his brother, thinking that everything will be fine once he gets home.

Analysis: Chapters 5–6

The Robert Frost poem Ponyboy recites to Johnny in Chapter 5, "Nothing Gold Can Stay," speaks of innocence by using metaphors from nature. The poem comes to symbolize the innocence of Johnny and Ponyboy. Not all of the greasers possess this innocence, and they long for Johnny and Ponyboy to retain theirs. The poem also suggests the impermanence of gold, pointing to the ending of the idyllic male bonding that Johnny and Ponyboy experience during their week of hiding out and foreshadowing the eventual end of their companionship.

In Chapter 5, the two young men talk and think extensively about what makes them the way they are. Ponyboy thinks about the honor code of the greasers, and suggests that they can be proud of their hair, if nothing else. When Johnny and Ponyboy cut their hair, which has long identified them as greasers, they symbolically shed their social identities. This partial freedom from their social category enables them to communicate more effectively and question the purpose behind their lifestyle. Johnny begins to think that greasers can take pride in their spirit and heritage, not just in their hair. He is finds the southern gentlemen in *Gone with the Wind* interesting, and he and Ponyboy begin to see their gang as a delinquent posse of southern gentlemen.

Ponyboy feels an increasing sense of membership in the greaser family, even adopting traits from his older counterparts. He begins to resemble Sodapop physically, and he makes wisecracks reminiscent of Two-Bit's. Dally's leather coat saves Ponyboy's life, signifying that Ponyboy thrives because his elders protect him. Finally, Ponyboy stops acting like a spoiled child and realizes that Darry is firm with him for his own good. Ponyboy realizes that the strength of the group lies in the solidarity of its members, and he begins learning to temper his individual needs for the sake of the group.

The events of Chapter 6 provide a mirror image of the events of Chapter 4. In murdering Bob, Johnny and Ponyboy make themselves criminals, and by saving children from a burning building, they make themselves heroes. When the two boys disobey Dally and run into the burning church, they further establish their agency and cement their independence from the older greasers. Moreover, their courageous rescue of the children from the burning church demonstrates that Hinton's greasers are not stereotypical hoods. Though they live in a harsh, uncertain, and violent world, Ponyboy, Johnny, and even Dally adhere to the values of courage and loyalty. The stereotypes that define the greasers' social class, Hinton asserts, do not define them as individuals.

Chapters 7–8

Summary: Chapter 7

> [G]reasers will still be greasers and Socs will still be Socs. Sometimes I think it's the ones in the middle that are really the lucky stiffs.
>
> (See QUOTATIONS, p. 40)

The reporters and police interview Ponyboy, Sodapop, and Darry in the hospital waiting room. Sodapop jokes with the reporters and hospital staff, keeping the mood light with his antics. The doctors finally emerge and say that Dally will be fine but that Johnny's back was broken when the roof caved in. Even if Johnny survives, they add, he will be permanently crippled.

The next morning, Ponyboy is making breakfast when Steve Randle (Sodapop's best friend) and Two-Bit come in with the morning papers. The papers portray Ponyboy, Johnny, and Dally as heroes for rescuing the schoolchildren. They also mention Ponyboy's excellent performance on the track team and in school. The papers mention that the state will charge Johnny with manslaughter and send both Ponyboy and Johnny to juvenile court, from which

Ponyboy might be sent to a boys' home. The other boys reassure Ponyboy that his family will stay together. Ponyboy tells them he had his recurring nightmare—which first occurred on the night of his parents' funeral—the previous night. He never remembers the dream, but it makes him wake up in intense panic.

Ponyboy asks Sodapop about Sandy and learns that she got pregnant and moved to Florida. Her parents refused to let her marry Sodapop because of his age, so Sandy left to live with her grandmother. Sodapop and Darry go to work, and Two-Bit and Ponyboy go to get Cokes at the Tasty Freeze. A blue Mustang pulls up to the restaurant, and in it they see the group of Socs that jumped Ponyboy and Johnny in the park. Ponyboy feels an immediate and intense hatred for them.

One of the Socs, Marcia's boyfriend, Randy, comes over to Ponyboy. Two-Bit reminds him that no fighting is allowed before the rumble, but Randy says he wants only to talk. He asks Ponyboy why he saved those children and says he would never have thought a greaser could do such a thing. Ponyboy says that it didn't have anything to do with his being a greaser. Sick about the violence and Bob's death, Randy says he does not intend to fight at the rumble. Randy explains that Bob was his best friend, a good guy with a terrible temper and overly indulgent parents. Ponyboy feels reassured by his talk with Randy and realizes that Socs can be human and vulnerable.

Summary: Chapter 8

We couldn't get along without him. We needed Johnny as much as he needed the gang. And for the same reason.

(See QUOTATIONS, p. 41)

Two-Bit and Ponyboy go to see Johnny and Dally in the hospital. Johnny, weak and pale, whispers that he would like Ponyboy to finish reading *Gone with the Wind* to him. His mother shows up to visit, but she is a mean-spirited, nagging woman and Johnny refuses to see her. As Ponyboy and Two-Bit leave, she accosts them and blames them for Johnny's condition, and Two-Bit insults her.

Dally is recovering nicely in the hospital, and for the first time ever Ponyboy feels warmly toward Dally. Dally says that Tim Shepard, the leader of another gang of greasers, came in to talk about the rumble. Dally asks for Two-Bit's black-handled switchblade, and

Two-Bit gladly hands over his prized possession without even asking why Dally needs it.

On the way home, Ponyboy and Two-Bit see Cherry Valance in her Corvette. She says that the Socs have agreed to fight with no weapons. Ponyboy asks her to go see Johnny, but she says she cannot because Johnny killed Bob. She says that Bob had a sweet side and was only violent when drunk, as he was when he beat up Johnny. Ponyboy calls her a traitor, but he quickly forgives her. He asks her if she can see the sunset on the West Side, and when she says she can, he tells her to remember that he can see it on the East Side too.

Analysis: Chapters 7–8

Family becomes increasingly important in the second half of the novel—both the biological Curtis family and the makeshift greaser family. Events begin to threaten the Curtis's cohesion, since a good chance exists that that state will take Ponyboy from his brothers and put him in a boys' home. This threat is especially heartrending for the brothers because Ponyboy is finally learning to appreciate Darry. It becomes important to Ponyboy to stay with his brothers as a matter of greaser pride. If the Curtis brothers can stay together, they can prove that greasers have the capability to overcome great odds and be functional, even successful.

For boys such as Johnny, fellow greasers are far more caring and stable than biological parents, and provide a more trustworthy family. His preference for the greasers and disdain for his dysfunctional family become evident when he allows Ponyboy and Two-Bit to visit him in the hospital but will not see his own mother. He refuses her, not because he is callous or because he wants to hurt her, but rather because he does not consider her an important part of his life. She has failed as a mother, denying him the nurturing that every child needs, and Ponyboy and Two-Bit have provided Johnny with an alternative source of support.

Ironically, the closer Johnny comes to death, the more he participates in his own life and considers his individual desires. He has long been involved with the greasers and led his life according to their principles, including disliking the Socs. Like a member of any group, however, Johnny needs an identity that is not wholly confined by the group to which he belongs. Being close to death affords Johnny a new perspective on life, one that is different from that of other greasers. He realizes not only that violence is futile but also, more important, that it doesn't have to make up his whole identity.

Ponyboy's conversations with the two Socs, Randy and Cherry, in this section emphasize his new appreciation of interpersonal connections—all people are individuals, as Ponyboy reminds Randy, while he reminds Cherry that the sunset can be seen just as well from the West Side as from the East Side. This discussion of the sunset illustrates yet another similarity between the two sides: no matter where one lives, whether one is a greaser or a Soc, one can still appreciate beauty. These conversations also allow an earlier topic to resurface, which is the discussion of cycles of nature that Ponyboy introduces through the Robert Frost poem. In this section, Ponyboy realizes that natural cycles, specifically life and death, apply to members of all social groups. This emphasis on commonality and connection occurs just as the characters are preparing for the rumble, their moment of sharpest division.

Chapters 9–10

Summary: Chapter 9

Stay gold, Ponyboy. Stay gold....

(See QUOTATIONS, p. 37)

Feeling sick before the rumble, Ponyboy swallows five aspirin and struggles to eat his dinner. The boys have bathed and made themselves look "tuff," and leave for the rumble excitedly. Ponyboy feels a sinking feeling when he sees the other greasers. Tim Shepard's gang and the others seem like genuine hoods. Twenty-two Socs arrive in four carloads to fight the twenty greasers. Darry steps forward to start the fight, and Paul Holden, Darry's high school friend and football teammate, steps up to challenge him. As Paul and Darry circle each other, Dally joins the group. As Dally arrives, the fight breaks out in full. After a long struggle, the greasers win.

When the rumble ends, Dally and Ponyboy go to the hospital to see Johnny. A policeman stops them, but Ponyboy feigns an injury, and the officer gives them an escort to the hospital. Ponyboy and Dally find Johnny dying. Johnny moans that fighting is useless, tells Ponyboy to "[s]tay gold," and then dies. Dally is beside himself with grief and runs frantically from the room.

Summary: Chapter 10

After Johnny's death, Ponyboy wanders alone for hours until a man offers him a ride. The man asks Ponyboy if he is okay and tells him that his head is bleeding. Ponyboy feels vaguely disoriented. At home, he finds the greasers gathered in the living room and tells them that Johnny is dead and that Dally has broken down. Dally calls and says he just robbed a grocery store and is running from the police. The gang rushes out and sees police officers chasing him. Dally pulls out the unloaded gun he carries, and the police shoot him. Dally collapses to the ground, dead. Ponyboy muses that Dally wanted to die. Feeling dizzy and overwhelmed, Ponyboy passes out.

When Ponyboy wakes, Darry is at his side. Ponyboy learns that he got a concussion when a Soc kicked him in the head during the rumble, and that he has been delirious in bed for three days.

Analysis: Chapters 9–10

Underlying the struggle between the Socs and the greasers is the struggle between the instinct to make peace and the social obligation to fight. Hinton turns the rumble into a moral lesson. The fight begins when Darry Curtis and Paul Holden face off; the fact that Darry and Paul were high school friends and football teammates suggests that their rivalry need not exist—that money makes enemies of natural friends. Ponyboy's comment that they used to be friends but now dislike each other because one has to work for a living while the other comes from the leisurely West Side emphasizes the artificial and unnecessary nature of their animosity. While this animosity seems pointless, each gang member who fights still feels a responsibility to his gang to hate the other gang.

Ponyboy feels this tension within him before the fight. His instincts tell him to skip the rumble, as he knows in his heart that violence won't solve anything. His hesitation after speaking with Randy and his decision to take five aspirin before the fight show that he is emotionally and physically unprepared for the ordeal. Nevertheless, Ponyboy ignores his instincts and goes through with the fight because he wants to please his social group. His participation in the rumble cements his place in the gang; he is no longer a tag-along little brother but rather a fighter in his own right.

The greasers prepare for the rumble as if preparing for a high school dance. They bathe, do their hair, and dress carefully. The rumble is a social event, an occasion to defend and celebrate one's identity. While other teenagers celebrate their identities by attending dances and parties, the greasers celebrate theirs by fighting. After the fight, however, the glamour of the event wears off. Despite their victory, the greasers understand the uselessness of violence. Nothing has really improved for them: greasers are injured, separation still threatens the Curtis brothers, and Johnny still lies dying.

Though everyone looks forward to the rumble as a culmination of tension, the rumble actually proves anticlimactic. Immediately after the rumble, Ponyboy and Dally rush to the hospital to see Johnny. Their actions suggests that the rumble is a minor event interrupting their real concerns. The rumble leaves the other greasers depressed too. Victory does not thrill them as they thought it would. The Socs retreat, but the greasers do not cheer. They bleed, double over, and examine their wounds. When Darry announces their victory, his voice is tired, not celebratory.

The events of these chapters mark the culmination of Ponyboy's trauma. Constant disaster has kept Ponyboy from feeling pain. Over the course of a few days, Ponyboy almost drowns, learns that his friend has committed murder, runs away and hides, saves children from a burning church, and learns that the state may take him away from his brothers. However, the emotions that surround these events have been pushed to the side by both by the constant onslaught of new trauma and by Ponyboy's worries about Johnny and the greaser-Soc rumble. Ponyboy's hospitalization suggests that the string of disasters has ended and that a period of reflection can finally begin.

CHAPTERS 11–12

SUMMARY: CHAPTER 11

Ponyboy is restricted to bed rest for a week after he wakes up from his concussion. He finds a picture of Bob the Soc in Sodapop's high school yearbook. Bob's grin reminds him of Sodapop's. Ponyboy wonders if Bob's parents hate him, saying he prefers their hatred to their pity. Looking at the photograph and remembering conversations with Cherry and Randy, Ponyboy concludes that Bob was cocky, hot-tempered, frightened, and human.

Randy arrives at the house to talk to Ponyboy and behaves with shocking insensitivity. Not thinking of what Ponyboy has suffered, Randy says he is worried about being associated with the violence.

They discuss the hearing scheduled for the next day. Ponyboy, in a delirious state, says that he killed Bob himself and that Johnny is still alive. Darry asks Randy to leave.

Summary: Chapter 12

Ponyboy does not have to speak much at the hearing, since his doctor has spoken to the judge about Ponyboy's condition. The judge asks Ponyboy a few gentle questions about his home life and then acquits him of all wrongdoing and allows him to return home with his brothers. After the hearing, Ponyboy becomes detached and depressed. His grades suffer, he loses his coordination, memory, and appetite, and he resumes fighting with Darry. Ponyboy's English teacher, Mr. Syme, says that although Ponyboy is failing, he can raise his grade to a C by writing an outstanding autobiographical theme.

The next day at lunch, Ponyboy goes to the grocery store with Steve and Two-Bit for candy bars and Cokes. When a group of Socs accosts him, he threatens them with a broken bottle, saying he refuses to take any more of their intimidation. Ponyboy's uncharacteristic show of hostility alarms Steve and Two-Bit, and they warn Ponyboy not to grow hard like Dally was. They are relieved when Ponyboy bends down to pick up the broken glass, not wanting anyone to get a flat tire.

That night as Ponyboy and Darry fight about Ponyboy's grades, Sodapop runs out of the house, upset that Sandy has returned a letter he wrote her unopened. Darry explains that Sodapop is not the father of Sandy's child and acts puzzled that Sodapop never told Ponyboy. Ponyboy reflects that he probably acted uninterested when Sodapop tried to talk about his problems. Worried, Darry and Ponyboy go find Sodapop. He tells them their constant fighting is tearing him apart. Sobbing, he asks them to try to understand each other and stop fighting. They promise to try. Ponyboy thinks that Sodapop will hold them together.

The boys run back home. Ponyboy looks at Johnny's copy of *Gone with the Wind*. He finds a handwritten note from Johnny urging him to stay gold and saying that the children's lives were worth his own. Ponyboy realizes that he wants to tell the story of his friends so that other hoodlums will not nurse their anger at the world and ignore the beauty in it. He begins to work on his English theme, starting with the words that begin *The Outsiders*: "When I stepped out into the bright sunlight from the darkness of the movie house, I had only two things on my mind: Paul Newman and a ride home."

Analysis: Chapters 11–12

At first, Ponyboy cannot come to terms with the deaths of Dally and Johnny. He is physically and emotionally immobilized. Even after he recovers from his physical injuries, he feels listless and empty, his grades slip, and his relationship with Darry suffers. Ponyboy's friends worry that he will cope by hardening into an angry hoodlum, a prospect that worries them. We might think that Ponyboy's shows of toughness would be a positive development in Steve and Two-Bit's eyes—displays like the one in the grocery store suggest that Ponyboy is losing his vulnerability to intimidation and thus becoming more valuable in the greaser gang. However, though it is important for a greaser to have a tough exterior, Ponyboy's friends do not want him to become something he is not. Because Johnny has died, Ponyboy is the last one of their group to retain the innocence that each group member lost but remembers with nostalgia. The greasers also worry about Ponyboy's show of toughness because they know that he is not naturally hostile or intimidating. The greasers' concern shows that they place as much importance on individual well-being as on group well-being. The consideration Ponyboy shows in picking up the broken glass from the bottle he uses to intimidate the Socs indicates that his capacity for angry outbursts is less a part of his character than his thoughtfulness and decency.

Ponyboy shows himself to be on the road to recovery when he hashes things out with his brothers. Though Ponyboy still feels the pain of loss, he can finally remember Johnny and Dally without feeling overwhelming denial or anguish. He begins to look at the plight of the greasers and juvenile delinquents with objectivity. He realizes that many boys his age hate the world and feel they must be tough and violent, and he begins to feel that someone should show them the good in the world. Ponyboy's decision to tell the greasers' story in his English theme paper marks his maturation into an emotionally capable young man. Hinton suggests that Ponyboy has found a way to make sense of the preventable violence in his life. Ponyboy's willingness to examine his painful past marks the last stage in his recovery and sets him up to achieve the potential that Darry has long seen in him.

That the novel's closing lines are an exact repetition of its opening lines symbolically initiates Ponyboy's exploration of his past through memory. With this exploration, recorded in Ponyboy's writing, we, as well as Ponyboy, finally discover a purpose to the seemingly senseless struggle that he has undergone. Hinton's act of ending the novel by circling back to its beginning provides a balanced symmetry to the story's structure. More important, however, Ponyboy's ability to tie the story up so neatly shows that he has dealt with these traumatic events in a healthy way.

Important Quotations Explained

1. Stay gold, Ponyboy. Stay gold.

As he lies dying in Chapter 9, Johnny Cade speaks these words to Ponyboy. "Stay gold" is a reference to the Robert Frost poem that Ponyboy recites to Johnny when the two hide out in the Windrixville Church. One line in the poem reads, "Nothing gold can stay," meaning that all good things must come to an end. By the end of the novel, the boys apply this idea to youthful innocence, believing that they cannot remain forever unsullied by the harsh realities of life. Here, Johnny urges Ponyboy to remain gold, or innocent. Johnny now senses the uselessness of fighting; he knows that Ponyboy is better than the average hoodlum, and he wants Ponyboy to hold onto the golden qualities that set him apart from his companions.

The quotation also recalls the period of time during which the boys' friendship blossoms and solidifies—the idyllic interlude at the church. During this blissful time, the two boys read, talk, and smoke, escaping the adult world of responsibility. Like the gold of the poem, however, this idyll is tinged with sadness. Just as the gold in the poem vanishes, the idyll must end, and the boys must face the consequences of the murder.

2. It's okay… We aren't in the same class. Just don't forget that some of us watch the sunset too.

Ponyboy speaks these words to Cherry Valance in Chapter 3 after he, Two-Bit, and Johnny spend time with Cherry and Marcia at the drive-in. Ponyboy points out that the sunset closes the gap between the greasers and Socs. He realizes that, even though the two groups have unequal lifestyles, attitudes, and financial situations, they nevertheless live in the same world, beneath the same sun. The words "some of us watch the sunset" suggest to Cherry that although some of the greasers live up to the stereotype of greasers as rough and unrefined, some of them, like Ponyboy, have a keen appreciation for beauty—as keen as that of the richest socialite. By agreeing on the basic fact that rich and poor people look at the same sun, Ponyboy and Cherry take a small step toward a potential reconciliation between the rival gangs. This moment of concord comes early in the narrative, and its idealistic tone makes the rifts and violence to come all the more painful.

3. Dally was so real he scared me.

Ponyboy speaks these words in Chapter 5, during his stay with Johnny in the abandoned church in Windrixville. Pony's realization stems from a comment Johnny makes after reading a passage from *Gone with the Wind,* in which he says that Dally reminds him of one of the gallant Southern gentlemen from the Civil War. The fact that Dally is too "real" for Ponyboy reveals something about his narrative perspective. He says earlier that the other greasers—Soda, Darry, and Two-Bit—remind him more of the heroes in his books than Dally does. Ponyboy feels more comfortable with Soda, Darry, and Two-Bit because as a narrator, and later a writer, he is more comfortable with fictional heroes than with real people like Dally who have lost their innocence.

Johnny, on the other hand, though quieter and more timid than Ponyboy, finds it in himself to admire Dally and to look past his intimidating exterior. Dally does not scare him but rather fascinates him, and he holds a romanticized vision of Dally as an honorable Southern gentleman. By comparing Dally to a character in a book, Johnny becomes able to understand him. In a sense, Ponyboy's and Johnny's comments about Dally reveal that Ponyboy is even more vulnerable than Johnny.

4. > Greasers will still be greasers and Socs will still be Socs. Sometimes I think it's the ones in the middle that are really the lucky stiffs.

Randy delivers these lines in Chapter 7 when he tells Ponyboy that he will not be fighting in the rumble. His words speak to an important idea in the novel—the futility of the recurring Soc-greaser violence. The idea Randy presents here has another side to it, however. By stating that the members of both groups will always remain in their respective groups, he suggests that it would be impossible for a greaser or a Soc to rise above his current status. He appears to believe that, despite their youth, the young men in the story will never be able to move on and transcend the narrow limits of their gang identities.

Randy's belief in the permanence of their social identities may be based, however, in the fact that he is a Soc and not a greaser. Having grown up in a wealthy and comfortable environment, it would not be difficult for him to imagine himself forever stuck in this lifestyle. A greaser, on the other hand, might have different ideas about social mobility. A poor youth from the East Side like Ponyboy would be more likely to imagine shedding the greaser lifestyle to pursue higher goals and improve his social status.

5. We couldn't get along without him. We needed Johnny as much as he needed the gang. And for the same reason.

This quotation comes from Chapter 8. As Ponyboy sits in the hospital and watches Johnny dying, he muses on the fragility of group cohesion. It seems obvious that Johnny needs the greasers—he is small, passive, and poor, which makes him an easy target of Soc violence. Less obvious is the gang's need for Johnny. The greasers need a vulnerable friend to give them a sense of purpose. Telling themselves that they exist to protect people like Johnny lets them avoid thinking about the fact that their poverty and vulnerability leave them no choice but to band together. Ponyboy comes to this conclusion at the end of the novel, as Johnny is dying. He understands Johnny's value only when he is about to lose Johnny, which amplifies the pain of the loss.

Key Facts

FULL TITLE
The Outsiders

AUTHOR
S. E. Hinton

TYPE OF WORK
Novel

GENRE
Coming-of-age; class struggle

LANGUAGE
English

TIME AND PLACE WRITTEN
1960s, Tulsa, Oklahoma

DATE OF FIRST PUBLICATION
1967

PUBLISHER
The Viking Press

NARRATOR
Ponyboy Curtis

POINT OF VIEW
Ponyboy gives a first-person, subjective account of events, explaining how we should interpret events and people in the story.

TONE
Youthful; melodramatic; slangy; simplistic

TENSE
Past

SETTING (TIME)
Mid-1960s

SETTING (PLACE)
Tulsa, Oklahoma

PROTAGONIST
Ponyboy

MAJOR CONFLICT
Against the background of the clash between the poor greasers and the rich Socs, the greaser Ponyboy struggles to mature.

RISING ACTION
Johnny kills a Soc; Johnny and Ponyboy flee; tension mounts between the greasers and Socs.

CLIMAX
Johnny's death, in Chapter 9.

FALLING ACTION
The greasers win the rumble; Dally dies; Ponyboy recovers from his emotional and physical trauma.

THEMES
Bridging the gap between rich and poor; honor among the lawless; the treacherousness of male-female interactions

MOTIFS
Literature; eye shape and color; Ponyboy's losses of consciousness

SYMBOLS
Two-Bit's switchblade; cars; Bob's rings; greaser hair

FORESHADOWING
The Socs jump Ponyboy while he walks home alone, previewing their later attack on him and Johnny; Johnny threatens to kill anybody who jumps him again, foreshadowing his murder of Bob.

Study Questions & Essay Topics

Study Questions

1. *Compare and contrast Johnny and Dally. What roles do they play in the novel? What roles do they play In Ponyboy's life?*

The Outsiders is a novel of conflicts—greaser against Soc, rich against poor, the desire for violence against the desire for reconciliation. Dally and Johnny do not battle against each other, but they are opposites. Johnny is meek, fearful, and childlike, while Dally is hard, cynical, and dangerous. As they near the ends of their lives, however, Johnny becomes strong and Dally becomes weak. Once-meek Johnny faces death with calm determination. He writes a strong, commanding note to Ponyboy, and he also transcends his meekness by refusing to see the mother who has always neglected him. Dally, on the other hand, is weakened by grief. He runs from Johnny's deathbed in a fit of uncontrollable sadness. In Ponyboy's view, Dally commits suicide by baiting the police and then showing them a gun, thus forcing the police to shoot him. Dally sheds his tough, cool exterior and reveals the fear that actually rules his behavior.

In Ponyboy's life, Dally and Johnny represent the qualities of innocence and strength that Ponyboy must reconcile. Dally and Johnny need one another. Johnny worships Dally's toughness and savvy, and Dally loves Johnny's vulnerability and openness, which remind him of the qualities he has lost after a lifetime on the street. Ponyboy realizes that he cannot become wholly naïve or wholly tough. He cannot stop being a greaser in order to retain his innocence or sacrifice his ideals in order to become a toughened gangster. He must learn how to be like both Dally and Johnny.

2. *Discuss Ponyboy's evolving conception of the Socs. How does his opinion of the Socs at the end of the novel differ from his opinion at the beginning?*

Over the course of the novel, Ponyboy's opinion of the Socs shifts. As his understanding of them changes, Ponyboy sees the Socs either in a negative light or more sympathetically. At the beginning of the novel, Ponyboy, like all of the greasers, hates and fears the Socs. He thinks of them as dangerous enemies. After he meets Cherry at the movie theater, however, Ponyboy begins to realize that Socs are human just like greasers. He sees that he and Cherry appreciate many of the same things, like sunsets. His empathy for the Socs suffers a setback, however, after a group of them attacks him and Johnny in the park.

When Ponyboy rescues the schoolchildren from the burning church, it opens him up to the idea of a human compassion that transcends gang loyalties. Later, Ponyboy talks with the Soc Randy about the rescue, and the two come to a peaceable understanding. Still, Ponyboy does not miraculously shed his animosity toward the Socs, not even after Johnny pleads with him to stop fighting. His traumatic experiences have scarred him. As the story ends, gang tensions still exist, and Ponyboy still feels anger. Yet he is about to embark upon an intelligent exploration of his tragedies by writing about them.

3. *How is "Nothing Gold Can Stay," the Robert Frost poem that Ponyboy recites to Johnny at the church, relevant to Ponyboy and Johnny's story?*

"Nothing Gold Can Stay" offers Ponyboy and Johnny a way to understand their lives; it gives the boys a framework for the traumatic events of their story. The poem likens the inevitable loss of innocence that the boys experience to the wilting of flowers. Sunrises transform the night into day, flowers wilt, and paradise is destroyed. In the poem, the conditions of existence dictate that everything loses its initial innocence. This loss of youth and purity does not have to be devastating, however. By using a metaphor from nature, Frost suggests that the loss of innocence is as natural as the death of a flower. Both losses must be accepted as an inevitable part of the cycle of life. Because of their poverty, the greasers will inevitably suffer losses and sacrifices. In citing the poem, Johnny and Ponyboy acknowledge that this loss is unavoidable but not that the loss of beauty is inevitable. Before he dies, Johnny urges Ponyboy to "[s]tay gold," to hold onto those ideals that will outlast his loss of youth and innocence.

Suggested Essay Topics

1. What draws Cherry to the greasers? Why is she with Bob? Why does she say she could fall in love with Dally?

2. Discuss the role of the novel's physical setting. How does the division between the East Side and the West Side represent the conflict within the novel itself?

3. Compare and contrast the Curtis brothers, Darry, Sodapop, and Ponyboy. How does their relationship change over the course of the novel?

4. Think about the role of physical violence in the novel. Is the violence shocking, predictable, boring, or melodramatic? Do you think such violence has a different effect on readers today than it did when the novel was first published?

Review & Resources

Quiz

1. Who is the second-youngest member of the greasers?

    A. Johnny
    B. Two-Bit
    C. Steve
    D. Sodapop

2. In which town is the abandoned church where Ponyboy and Johnny hide out located?

    A. Tonkawa
    B. Guthrie
    C. Windrixville
    D. Bartlesville

3. In which sport does Ponyboy participate?

    A. Football
    B. Track
    C. Wrestling
    D. Gymnastics

4. What is the name of Sodapop's horse?

    A. Daniel
    B. Captain Steve
    C. Lightning
    D. Mickey Mouse

5. What does Ponyboy say is visible on both the East Side and the West Side?

    A. Sunsets
    B. Rainbows
    C. Sunrises
    D. The moon

6. What book do Johnny and Ponyboy read in the church?

    A. *How the West Was Won*
    B. *Rumble Fish*
    C. *Gone with the Wind*
    D. *Great Expectations*

7. Who kills Dally?

    A. Darry
    B. The police
    C. Bob and Randy
    D. A drunk driver

8. How does Darry know Paul Holden, his first opponent at the rumble?

    A. They played football together in high school.
    B. Paul jumped Darry once.
    C. Paul brought his car to the garage where Darry works.
    D. Darry dated Paul's sister.

9. Who is Randy?

    A. A greaser from an enemy gang
    B. A Soc who refuses to fight in the rumble
    C. One of Ponyboy's high school teachers
    D. None of the above

10. Why does Sodapop's girlfriend Sandy move to Florida?

    A. To go to college
    B. Because her parents are moving
    C. Because she is wanted by the police
    D. Because she is pregnant

11. Who is the father of Sandy's baby?

    A. It is not revealed.
    B. Sodapop
    C. Paul Holden
    D. Mr. Syme

12. With what does Ponyboy threaten the Socs who approach him outside of the convenience store?

    A. A switch-blade
    B. A gun
    C. A broken pop bottle
    D. An arrest warrant

13. How does Ponyboy get a concussion?

    A. A roof beam falls on him during the fire.
    B. A Soc hits him with a lead pipe.
    C. He is kicked in the head during the rumble.
    D. He falls down a staircase in the fire.

14. Which character dies first?

    A. Johnny
    B. Bob
    C. Dally
    D. Nobody dies

15. Who is Randy's girlfriend?

    A. Cherry
    B. Sandy
    C. Julia
    D. Marcia

16. Which character has movie-star good looks?

    A. Sodapop
    B. Two-Bit
    C. Darry
    D. Cherry

17. What is Two-Bit's most prized possession?

    A. His 1920 silver dollar
    B. His silver-plated .45
    C. His black-handled switchblade
    D. His mother's locket

18. How old is Darry?

    A. Twenty-three
    B. Twenty
    C. Nineteen
    D. Eighteen

19. Why are Cherry and Marcia alone at the drive-in?

    A. Their boyfriends left because they did not like the movies that were playing.
    B. Their boyfriends walked off with two other girls from their high school.
    C. The girls decided to go out by themselves that day.
    D. The girls walked away from their boyfriends when they found out their boyfriends had booze.

20. When did Ponyboy's recurring nightmares begin?

    A. The night of his parents' funeral
    B. The night Johnny killed Bob
    C. The night he found out Sodapop was dropping out of school
    D. The night he met Cherry Valance

21. What kind of car does Cherry drive?

    A. A Mustang
    B. A Corvette
    C. A Volkswagon
    D. A Ferrari

22. Who bleaches Ponyboy's hair?

    A. Sodapop
    B. Marcia
    C. Johnny
    D. Dally

23. How did the Curtis brothers' parents die?

    A. In a car accident
    B. In a roller-coaster accident
    C. In a boating accident
    D. In a horse-riding accident

24. What is Ponyboy's real name?

    A. Frederick
    B. Walter
    C. Jason
    D. Ponyboy

25. Where did Dally live right before moving to Ponyboy's town?

    A. New Orleans
    B. Dallas
    C. New York
    D. Tuscaloosa

Answer Key:
1: A; 2: C; 3: B; 4: D; 5: A; 6: C; 7: B; 8: A; 9: B; 10: D; 11: A; 12: C; 13: C; 14: B; 15: D; 16: A; 17: C; 18: B; 19: D; 20: A; 21: B; 22: C; 23: A; 24: D; 25: C

Suggestions for Further Reading

DALY, JAY. *Presenting S. E. Hinton.* Boston: Twayne Author Series, 1989.

FORSTER, H. M. "A Book, a Place, a Time: Using Young Adult Novels in a Reading Workshop." *English Journal 84, no. 5* (1995): 115–119.

HARRIS, LAURIE, ED. *Biography Today: Profiles of People of Interest to Young Readers* (Author Series, Vol. 1). Detroit: Omnigraphics, 1995.

HINTON, S.E. *Rumble Fish.* New York: Delacorte, 1975.

———. *Tex.* New York: Delacorte, 1980.

———. *That Was Then, This Is Now.* New York: Viking, 1971.

KOVACS, DEBORAH, ED. *Meet the Authors: 25 Writers of Upper Elementary and Middle School Books Talk about Their Work.* New York: Scholastic, 1996.

MIKLOWITZ, GLORIA. *The War Between the Classes.* New York: Laurel Leaf, 1986.

A Note on the Type

The typeface used in SparkNotes study guides is Sabon, created by master typographer Jan Tschichold in 1964. Tschichold revolutionized the field of graphic design twice: first with his use of asymmetrical layouts and sanserif type in the 1930s when he was affiliated with the Bauhaus, then by abandoning assymetry and calling for a return to the classic ideals of design. Sabon, his only extant typeface, is emblematic of his latter program: Tschichold's design is a recreation of the types made by Claude Garamond, the great French typographer of the Renaissance, and his contemporary Robert Granjon. Fittingly, it is named for Garamond's apprentice, Jacques Sabon.

SparkNotes Test Preparation Guides

The SparkNotes team figured it was time to cut standardized tests down to size. We've studied the tests for you, so that SparkNotes test prep guides are:

Smarter:
Packed with critical-thinking skills and test-taking strategies that will improve your score.

Better:
Fully up to date, covering all new features of the tests, with study tips on every type of question.

Faster:
Our books cover exactly what you need to know for the test. No more, no less.

SparkNotes Guide to the SAT & PSAT
SparkNotes Guide to the SAT & PSAT — Deluxe Internet Edition
SparkNotes Guide to the ACT
SparkNotes Guide to the ACT — Deluxe Internet Edition
SparkNotes Guide to the SAT II Writing
SparkNotes Guide to the SAT II U.S. History
SparkNotes Guide to the SAT II Math Ic
SparkNotes Guide to the SAT II Math IIc
SparkNotes Guide to the SAT II Biology
SparkNotes Guide to the SAT II Physics

SAT and PSAT are registered trademarks of the College Entrance Examination Board, which does not endorse these books.
ACT is a registered trademark of ACT, Inc. which neither sponsors nor endorses these books.

SparkNotes Study Guides:

- 1984
- The Adventures of Huckleberry Finn
- The Adventures of Tom Sawyer
- The Aeneid
- All Quiet on the Western Front
- And Then There Were None
- Angela's Ashes
- Animal Farm
- Anne of Green Gables
- Antony and Cleopatra
- As I Lay Dying
- As You Like It
- The Awakening
- The Bean Trees
- The Bell Jar
- Beloved
- Beowulf
- Billy Budd
- Black Boy
- Bless Me, Ultima
- The Bluest Eye
- Brave New World
- The Brothers Karamazov
- The Call of the Wild
- Candide
- The Canterbury Tales
- Catch-22
- The Catcher in the Rye
- The Chosen
- Cold Mountain
- Cold Sassy Tree
- The Color Purple
- The Count of Monte Cristo
- Crime and Punishment
- The Crucible
- Cry, the Beloved Country
- Cyrano de Bergerac
- Death of a Salesman
- The Diary of a Young Girl
- Doctor Faustus
- A Doll's House
- Don Quixote
- Dr. Jekyll and Mr. Hyde
- Dracula
- Dune
- Emma
- Ethan Frome
- Fahrenheit 451
- Fallen Angels
- A Farewell to Arms
- Flowers for Algernon
- The Fountainhead
- Frankenstein
- The Glass Menagerie
- Gone With the Wind
- The Good Earth
- The Grapes of Wrath
- Great Expectations
- The Great Gatsby
- Gulliver's Travels
- Hamlet
- The Handmaid's Tale
- Hard Times
- Harry Potter and the Sorcerer's Stone
- Heart of Darkness
- Henry IV, Part I
- Henry V
- Hiroshima
- The Hobbit
- The House of the Seven Gables
- I Know Why the Caged Bird Sings
- The Iliad
- Inferno
- Invisible Man
- Jane Eyre
- Johnny Tremain
- The Joy Luck Club
- Julius Caesar
- The Jungle
- The Killer Angels
- King Lear
- The Last of the Mohicans
- Les Misérables
- A Lesson Before Dying
- The Little Prince
- Little Women
- Lord of the Flies
- Macbeth
- Madame Bovary
- A Man for All Seasons
- The Mayor of Casterbridge
- The Merchant of Venice
- A Midsummer Night's Dream
- Moby-Dick
- Much Ado About Nothing
- My Ántonia
- Mythology
- Native Son
- The New Testament
- Night
- The Odyssey
- The Oedipus Trilogy
- Of Mice and Men
- The Old Man and the Sea
- The Old Testament
- Oliver Twist
- The Once and Future King
- One Flew Over the Cuckoo's Nest
- One Hundred Years of Solitude
- Othello
- Our Town
- The Outsiders
- Paradise Lost
- The Pearl
- The Picture of Dorian Gray
- A Portrait of the Artist as a Young Man
- Pride and Prejudice
- The Prince
- A Raisin in the Sun
- The Red Badge of Courage
- The Republic
- Richard III
- Robinson Crusoe
- Romeo and Juliet
- The Scarlet Letter
- A Separate Peace
- Silas Marner
- Sir Gawain and the Green Knight
- Slaughterhouse-Five
- Snow Falling on Cedars
- The Sound and the Fury
- Steppenwolf
- The Stranger
- A Streetcar Named Desire
- The Sun Also Rises
- A Tale of Two Cities
- The Taming of the Shrew
- The Tempest
- Tess of the d'Urbervilles
- Their Eyes Were Watching God
- Things Fall Apart
- To Kill a Mockingbird
- To the Lighthouse
- Treasure Island
- Twelfth Night
- Ulysses
- Uncle Tom's Cabin
- Walden
- Wuthering Heights
- A Yellow Raft in Blue Water